Mini Mysteries

20 Tricky Tales to Untangle

By Rick Walton
Illustrated by Lauren Scheuer

⭐ American Girl™

D0041375

Printed in China.
11 12 13 14 15 LEO 29 28 27 26 25
All American Girl marks are trademarks of American Girl.
Editorial Development: Trula Magruder, Judith Lary
Art Direction & Design: Chris David
Production: Mindy Rappe, Kendra Pulvermacher, Jeannette Bailey
Illustrations: Lauren Scheuer

Dear Reader,

Do you like to crack cases? Uncover clues? Identify suspects? Look inside! You'll find a year of mini mysteries waiting for a super sleuth like you.

Read the story and then try to figure out the whodunit along with Marie and her pals. But beware of red herrings—those false leads that can send you in the wrong direction.

Once you think you've found a solution, open the case-closed folder in back to check your answer.

Happy sleuthing!

Your friends at American Girl

MARIE

Contents

NOELLE

HAILEY

BROOKE

HoPE

MeGAN

Sage

FAith

Rose

Wishing for Change

Is there a thief at the zoo? Or is a very clean kid in the wrong spot at the wrong time?

"Aw," said Marie Cantu. "Too bad we can't feed the polar bears. They're so cute!"

The zoo had a few wild animals that the signs made clear you were to look at and not feed.

"They are cute, but I don't think you want to get that close to them," said Noelle Dee, her best friend and next-door neighbor.

The two were spending a Saturday afternoon at Liberty Park Zoo. It wasn't a huge zoo, but it wasn't bad for a town the size of theirs. The best thing about the zoo was that there were so many things to do. You could scurry through tunnels like a gopher; pet baby goats, sheep, and rabbits; and make wishes at a fountain where the water shot high into the air and danced.

There even were a few animals you *could* feed. Next to an animal's habitat was a vending machine with food prepared especially for that animal—rabbit and deer pellets, birdseed, fish food, and crackers for the ducks. If you didn't have the dimes or quarters that the food machines took, you could always get change for your dollars at the food court change machines.

The girls had seen the big animals, wrinkled their noses at the smell, gone through the snake den, and now stood in front of the deer habitat. "Do you have any change?" Marie asked. The girls loved feeding the deer, which would eat right out of their hands.

"Don't I always?" Noelle reached into her pocket, pulled out a couple of quarters, and gave one to Marie, who headed for the deer food machine.

But a boy beat her to it. He reached into his pocket and pulled out a handful of shiny change—quarters, dimes, nickels, and lots of pennies. Noelle looked closely. That was odd. The money wasn't shiny new; it was shiny wet!

The boy took a quarter and reached toward the coin slot. But before he could put it in, a large hand touched his shoulder. "Just a minute," said a zoo employee. "I don't think that money belongs to you."

"Does too," said the boy.

"I think not," the employee said. "You took it from the fountain. We have witnesses who say they saw you."

"They're wrong," replied the boy. "I got this money from the change machine."

The employee turned to Marie and Noelle. "Is he with you?"

"Yes," said the boy. He pointed at Noelle, whose dark curls were something like his own. "She's my sister. She'll tell you that I'm not lying." He whispered to Noelle, "Say yes and I'll give you a quarter."

"He's *not* my brother," said Noelle.

"We've never seen him before," Marie agreed.

The boy laughed. "Sisters, always trying to get you into trouble. C'mon, Sis, tell the man who I am." And then he whispered to Noelle, "Two quarters."

"Ask him why his coins are wet," said Marie.

"That's easy," said the boy. "Whenever I get coins from a machine, I wash them. Don't you? You never know what germs are on them."

"Did you get all of those coins from the change machine?" Marie asked.

"Of course," said the boy. "I already told you I did."

Marie turned to the zoo employee. "I don't know if he took those coins from the fountain. I suspect he did, since they're wet. But I can prove he didn't get them from the change machine."

Wishing for
Change

How did Marie prove the boy was lying?
You can't change the truth. See page 81.

Behind the Door

Someone's vandalized the rest room doors at the mall. How will the girls figure out which one to enter?

"Let's see, according to the mall map, the rest rooms should be down this way and to the left," Marie said to Noelle and headed off. The girls were at the mall shopping for a birthday present for Marie's mom.

They followed the map to a small hallway and turned down it. "Here they are," said Marie. "There's the MEN's room, and here's the ... ME room? Where's the WOMEN's room?"

The door on the left had MEN printed on it in large black letters. The door on the right had just ME. Both doors were scratched up pretty badly.

Noelle shook her head. "I guess I'm a me and you're a me. Just in case, let's go in the ME door together." They both put their hands on the ME door, but Marie suddenly pulled back. She looked again at both doors.

"I'm not sure," said Marie. "I don't want to surprise anybody. We'd better go ask."

The store next to the rest rooms was a Pretzel Baker. Noelle and Marie headed for the counter. A faint smell of chocolate and cinnamon and a strong smell of fresh bread dough swirled around them. "What can I get you girls?" asked the woman behind the counter. "My favorite's the cinnamon sugar. But we have a fresh batch of chocolate chip pretzels out of the oven, and they're to die for!"

Noelle pulled a few dollars out of her pocket and looked questioningly at Marie. The pretzels did look good, but Marie had other matters on her mind. "Maybe later," she said. "We need some help. These rest rooms right around the corner— which is the men's and which is the women's?"

Noelle added, "Is the women's room the one that says MEN or the one that says ME?"

"Haven't they fixed those yet?" asked the pretzel lady. "The doors were vandalized yesterday. I heard that someone scraped letters off both doors. Maintenance said they'd get right on it, but I guess they're a little slow."

"Yeah, the doors are pretty bad," said Marie. "So, is the women's room the one on the left or the one on the right?"

"It's the one on the . . . oh . . . I'm sorry, I've been working here for only two days. I can't remember which is which right now. I've never even been in them. We have our own rest room in back. Go ask at the jewelry store next door. The saleswoman there has been around a long time. She'll know."

"Thanks," said Marie. She turned to head toward the jewelry store. Then she stopped. She looked again at the pretzel lady and smiled. "Thanks. You've been a great help. I know which door is the one to the women's room now."

Marie headed back to the rest rooms with Noelle close behind. She carefully pushed open one of the doors and shouted, "Anybody in there?"

There was no answer.

She went all the way in. Then she shouted out, "Come on in, Noelle. I was right. This is it."

Behind the Door

Which door did Marie go through, and how did she know which room was the women's rest room?

Scratching your head? See page 81.

Play with Your Feud

Just before opening night, the stars of the play refuse to look at each other. Will the show ever go on?

The rehearsal for the spring play wasn't going well.

The scenery wasn't ready. Some of the actors didn't have all their lines memorized. Nerves were getting frayed.

And then things blew up.

"I will not work with Sage!" said Hope Harrison.

"And I won't talk to Hope!" added Sage Matthews.

This was quite a problem. Hope and Sage were the stars of the play *The Pet Shop,* which parents, teachers, and students would all turn out to see tomorrow night!

"That's just great," groaned Matt Thompson. He scratched at his hot, furry costume. "How can we rehearse? Girls—"

"—Girls, girls," interjected Mrs. Mahoney, the play's director. "Calm down. Let's be nice and get back to work. Oh, I hate it when you fight!"

Mrs. Mahoney had been the spring play's volunteer director ever since her first child had entered Lincoln Middle School thirty-five years ago. Even after her last child had graduated, she kept directing. She was a sweet lady, patient with the students and a good play director, but she was horrible at resolving conflicts.

"I refuse to rehearse if I have to look at Sage," said Hope.

"Fine with me," said Sage. "I hope I never have to see you again!" She swung around and her long mouse tail followed.

"Girls, girls," said Mrs. Mahoney. "Please."

But Hope and Sage, cat and mouse, crossed their arms and glared—away from each other.

"Come on, you're wasting our time," Matt said. "This costume is getting really hot!"

"Grow up, you two," said Megan Brown, walking from behind a giant goldfish bowl to center stage. "I have a line and I want to get it over with! Rehearse with your eyes closed."

"I'd keep my eyes closed," said Sage, "but I don't trust Hope to keep hers closed, and I don't want her looking at me!"

"Please, ladies," said Mrs. Mahoney, her arms filled with various headbands decorated to look like a bunny, a puppy, and a guinea pig. "You're actors. Pretend you like each other!"

Noelle could feel the tension on the stage, which resembled a giant pet shop. "Rehearse back-to-back!" she suggested.

"She would back into me just to crush my tail," said Sage.

"We'll blindfold you," said Megan.

"That would mess up my ears," replied Hope, adjusting the pointed black felt.

"Let's just replace them," sighed Matt, tugging at the zipper on the front of his spotted suit.

"Oh dear, we can't do that," said Mrs. Mahoney. "The play's tomorrow night, and they're the only ones who know their lines. Oh, what are we going to do?"

"Mrs. Mahoney?" Marie stepped up. "I know how Sage and Hope can face each other, keep their eyes open, and practice without looking at each other or touching each other."

"We can't turn off the lights," said Mrs. Mahoney. "That would be too dangerous."

"We won't turn off the lights," said Marie.

"Then go ahead," said Mrs. Mahoney. "Right now I'm willing to try almost anything."

"Sage? Hope? Close your eyes," said Marie.

"They're already closed," snapped Hope.

Marie took Sage and moved her up near the front of the stage. She turned Sage's back to the audience. "Don't back up," said Marie, "or you'll take an unhappy trip."

Marie then took Hope and moved her so that she was standing six feet in front of Sage, facing her.

"There!" Marie smiled. "Noelle, are you ready?"

"Ready!"

"GO!" shouted Marie.

A few seconds later, Marie spoke to the girls. "Open your eyes and get back to rehearsing!"

Play with Your Feud

What did Marie do so that Hope and Sage could practice without looking at each other?
Play detective, then see page 81.

An Elephant for President?

Someone's trying to ruin Marie and Noelle's campaign. Could it be . . . the boys?

The campaign poster showed an elephant with a girl's head on it. A long trunk stretched out from the girl's head. The caption read, "Vote for Marie Cantu—she *nose* what to do."

Marie admitted it was a clever idea, but she really *was* planning to run for student body president, and this silly poster could hurt her chances.

"Cute," said Noelle. "I've never seen a blond elephant."

"Let me show you something really bad." Noelle dragged Marie down the hall to another taped-up poster. This one had a hippopotamus with Noelle's head on it. Noelle's long curly brown hair hung to the ground.

This campaign slogan said, "Hippo-Hippo-Hurray! Noelle Dee for Lincoln Middle School Vice President!"

"That is bad," Marie said. "They're all over the school. Everyone's seen them!"

"Who do you think did it?" asked Noelle.

"I have no idea, but it's someone who doesn't want us—"

"—elected." Noelle broke in, finishing Marie's sentence as she often did. The girls dropped their notebooks to take the posters down, but just then the bell rang. School was starting. The posters would have to wait.

At morning recess, Marie and Noelle grabbed three of their friends—Rose James, Sage Matthews, and Faith Peterson—to help take down posters. But as they walked up and down the halls, they found that the posters were already gone.

"Did you see them?" asked Marie.

"Everybody saw them," said Faith.

"Thank goodness the custodian took them down."

"Too bad," said Faith. "I wanted one as a souvenir. They were funny."

The girls talked as they walked out to the playground.

"They *were* funny," said Noelle, "but they might cost Marie and me the election. We want to find out who put them up."

"Probably one of the boys," said Sage.

"Possibly," added Marie. "But it looks like the poster maker knew we were planning to run, and we've told only a few friends."

"Couldn't have been me," said Sage. "I'm not a good enough artist to have made those posters. Rose, you're a great artist. You could have made the posters."

Rose flipped her dark brown hair defiantly. "I've been staying with my grandma all week, and all my art supplies are at home, so I couldn't have made the posters."

"What posters?" Hope Harrison asked as she walked up to the group.

"Where've you been?" asked Sage. "*The* posters. They were plastered all over the school. Of Marie and Noelle running for president and vice president."

"I just got back from the dentist. Haven't been to school yet. So, you have your posters up already?" asked Hope. "Cool! I've been thinking of running myself, but I'll just vote for you two instead. Then, when you win, you can make me secretary of state or something."

"They're joke posters," said Rose. "Someone put Marie and Noelle's heads on animals' pictures. We're trying to find out who made them."

Marie crossed her arms. "Maybe you *should* run, Hope. Everyone's seen these posters, and they might have ruined our chances at winning. So it might as well be you. Then, when you win, you can make me ambassador to France."

"Oh, you'll still win," said Hope.

Marie wasn't sure she had as much confidence that she and Noelle would win as Hope had. "Let's get back to the mystery. Who would have put up those posters?"

"Faith," said Rose, "you've been really quiet. Where were you this morning?"

"I was right behind you, walking to school. You saw me. And no, I didn't make the posters."

Hope leaned over to Sage. "I wish I could have seen the posters. Were they really funny? Who was on the hippo?"

"Noelle was on the hippo," answered Sage. "Marie was on the elephant." And then Sage whispered, "And yes, the posters were funny. I still think it was one of the boys."

"There's a lot we can blame them for," said Marie. "But not this." She smiled at Noelle. "Should we tell them who did it?"

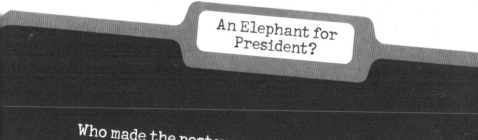

An Elephant for President?

Who made the posters, and how did Marie know?
Find out on page 81.

Rock and Rumors

It looks like two best friends are planning separate sleepovers. Looks can be deceiving.

"I heard you and Noelle will rule Lincoln next year," Megan said to Marie as the two girls walked slowly down Ivy Street on a beautiful spring day.

Megan Brown was two years older and a little taller than Marie.

"Yeah," said Marie modestly. "Hope's campaign was brilliant. We won in a landslide. Our biggest problem was that people kept taking our campaign posters for souvenirs."

"Just think," said Megan, "your face will be on the bedroom walls of all the cute Lincoln boys."

Megan was into boys. Perhaps it was because she was older, or perhaps because she didn't have any brothers. Marie had three brothers (one older, two younger), and they drove her nuts.

"My face on an elephant's body," said Marie. "That's really attractive, isn't it?"

The girls walked and chatted, enjoying the sun. Once Marie thought she heard someone calling her, and she turned to see Hailey Ferris behind her, headphones on, a CD player in hand, humming to a familiar song. Hailey looked up and waved.

Hailey continued to walk behind the girls for a few more minutes. Then, as soon as she had a chance, she turned a corner, leaving the girls alone.

Hailey had seen enough. She raced over to Noelle's house. "I tell you, Noelle," said Hailey, "they're planning a slumber party! Just the two of them. I was right behind them and heard them talking about it."

Noelle had been reading on her front porch when Hailey had walked up. Noelle kept reading as Hailey talked.

"It's this Friday. They're not going to invite you. Marie said she likes Megan because she's older and more mature."

Noelle slammed her book shut. She hated to admit that she was jealous, but she was.

She and Marie had grown up next door to each other. They'd been best friends forever. Marie was the only girl in a family of three boys, and Noelle was the only girl in a family of four boys. Marie was the sister Noelle had never had, and she thought Marie felt the same way about her.

"Marie is her own person," said Noelle. "She can have a slumber party and be friends with whoever she wants."

"Hey," said Hailey, "let's have our own slumber party."

Noelle put down her book. She didn't feel like reading anymore. "We'll see. I need to go clean up for dinner. See ya, Hailey."

Hailey waved good-bye and dashed for home—and the phone.

"Marie? This is Hailey."

Marie was surprised to hear Hailey on the other end of the line. Hailey had lived in the neighborhood for a couple of years and was in the same grade, but she'd never hung out with Marie—and Hailey had never called her before. "Oh hi, Hailey."

"Noelle and I are having a sleepover this Friday, just the two of us," said Hailey. "And she said you and Megan can have your own sleepover."

Marie was quiet for a moment. Then she said, "Hailey, can you come to my house and tell me more about the sleepover?"

When Hailey arrived at Marie's, she was surprised to see Noelle there, too.

"O.K., Hailey, what's going on?" Marie asked. "I called Noelle and she told me that she didn't say she'd have a sleepover with you."

"And Marie told me she's not planning a sleepover with Megan," Noelle added.

"Uh . . . but I heard them talking about it, Noelle," said Hailey. "I was walking behind them. You even turned and saw me, didn't you, Marie?"

"You were there," said Marie. "But you didn't hear what you say you heard, and I can prove it."

Rock and Rumors

How did Marie prove that Hailey wasn't telling the truth? Find the honest answer on page 81.

Up, Up, and A-What?

Noelle discovers a message while floating in a hot-air balloon. But what does the message mean?

"You're going to love it," gushed Hailey. "It's not scary at all!"

"We'll see about that," said Marie, who was afraid of heights.

It was the day of the big balloon festival. Dozens of hot-air balloonists had come from all over the country to fly their balloons.

One of those balloonists was Carol Ferris, Hailey's mom. Mrs. Ferris had told Hailey she could invite a couple of friends to take a ride. Hailey had invited Marie and Noelle.

"Are you sure there's room for all of us?" asked Marie, sizing up the small basket. "If there's not, I could stay down here, and you all could go up."

"There's plenty of room," said Mrs. Ferris.

"How about your other girls?" Marie asked. "Don't they want to go riding with their mom?"

"My daughters have been up with me a thousand times."

"At least," Hailey added.

"Besides, they said they have a project to do this morning," said Mrs. Ferris.

"I think that project is watching cartoons in their pajamas," Hailey whispered to Marie and Noelle.

"So, climb in, girls," said Mrs. Ferris, "and we'll be off into the wild blue." Hailey stepped into the basket and then moved to the back to give Noelle and Marie room. Noelle climbed in, smiling. She loved to fly but had never done anything so adventurous as this! Marie hesitated outside the basket until Noelle reached out to help her in.

"She's just nervous," explained Noelle. To Marie she said, "Don't worry. I'll hold on to you."

"I was nervous the first time I went up in a balloon, too," said Mrs. Ferris. "But you get used to it. Besides, no one's ever fallen out of *my* basket."

"I wasn't nervous my first time," said Hailey.

"You were two years old your first time," replied Mrs. Ferris. "You didn't know any better."

Hailey's mom showed Marie and Noelle what to hold on to and explained how the balloon worked. Then slowly, gently, they began to rise.

"If you open your eyes, you'll enjoy it more," Noelle said to Marie. "This is incredible!"

Marie held on tightly to the basket and slowly opened her eyes. It *was* incredible. She peered down as the earth fell away below her and the cars, the people, everything grew smaller and smaller. She watched in awe as they passed over the McDonald's next to the launch field, over the grocery store her parents shopped at, over streets, houses, and fields.

"Look," said Noelle, pointing down at the field over which they were flying. "I see a bunch of letters."

Below them someone had formed, with sheets and blankets, five huge letters: W O W I H.

"Someone's excited," said Hailey.

"Yeah," said Mrs. Ferris. "I wonder what it means?"

"It's a message, Mrs. Ferris," said Marie. "And it's for you."

Up, Up, and A-What?

How does Marie know the message is for Mrs. Ferris, and what does it mean?

Get the whole story on page 81.

The Original Boston Brooke

No one expected to hear such an amazing story from the new girl. But is it the truth or a big fat lie?

It was Saturday morning, and the first thing the people on Ivy Street noticed when they went outside was the moving van parked at the old Benson house.

Soon people began to gather. Some came to help carry in couches, tables, beds, an organ. Some came just to meet their new neighbors. But the kids arrived to see if there was anyone new their own age. For some of the girls, there was.

"My name's Marie," said Marie, and she stuck out her hand to the new girl. "This is Noelle and Hailey and Megan."

"Hi! I'm Brooke. Brooke Pinnock."

Suddenly questions started to fly.

"Where did you used to live?" asked Noelle.

"Boston."

"What grade are you in?"

"Fifth."

"What do your parents do?" Noelle had lots of questions.

"My parents aren't alive. I live with my grandparents. Grandpa just retired, and Grandma and Grandpa wanted to move to a smaller town. So here we are."

"Do you have any older brothers?" This was from Megan.

"Nope," said Brooke. "Do you?"

Megan shook her head no.

"What did your grandpa do before he retired?" asked Marie.

Brooke smiled. "He played for the Boston Red Sox."

Silence. And then Noelle asked, "Your grandpa played for the Boston Red Sox?"

"Sure," said Brooke. "He was good. The best. He also played for the Yankees, the White Sox, the Tigers, the Blue Jays—at one time or another, he played for every team in the American

League. He played for forty years!"

"No one can play for that long," said Hailey.

"Grandpa did."

"It's too physical," insisted Megan. "He'd burn out long before forty years were up."

"He did complain about arthritis in his fingers toward the end," said Brooke. "But besides that, he didn't seem to have much of a problem."

Megan stepped closer to Brooke. "Look, you don't have to lie to us—"

"I think she's just joking," said Hailey, giving the new girl a chance to change her story.

Brooke smiled and folded her arms. "Grandpa played for the Boston Red Sox. I'll bet anyone ten dollars that I'm telling the truth."

"I'll take that bet," said Megan.

"Hey, you don't *have* ten dollars—" started Noelle.

"—Me too!" interrupted Hailey.

"Wait a minute," said Marie suddenly. "I wouldn't take that bet if I were you. Brooke's telling the truth. Her grandfather did play for the Red Sox, and for every American League team. Brooke just left out one important detail."

The Original
Boston Brooke

What detail did Brooke leave out?
Get the juicy details on page 83.

Wave Good-Bye

A boy's snorkeling gear is missing.
Did someone in Marie's family take it?

"I told you getting up early would be worth it," Marie's dad said.

It was. The family and Noelle had the beach to themselves.
The only sounds were the caws of sea birds and the shouts of
Marie's three brothers as they dove into the cold ocean. O.K., so
it wasn't as peaceful as it could have been, but it was still nice.

"Let's move here," said Marie. "Then we can go to the beach every morning instead of for just a few days during our vacation."

Marie's mom laughed. "When you're rich and famous, Marie, you can buy a beach house and invite us."

Marie's parents began clearing away seaweed left from last night's high tide so that they'd have room to set up camp.

"Want us to help?" Marie asked.

"You girls go jump in the water," replied Mr. Cantu, "or build a sandcastle or dig for clams or something. Go have fun. We're fine here."

"Let's go beachcombing," Marie said to Noelle. "We can see what the tide brought in."

Noelle, who'd been invited on the Cantu family vacation, headed along the beach with Marie to go treasure hunting.

"A sand dollar!" shouted Marie. It was in perfect shape.

"Here's another," said Noelle.

The girls picked up treasures as they found them—a couple of broken conch shells, more sand dollars, some sea-polished stones, and a few pretty driftwood pieces.

"I have all I can carry," said Noelle.

"Me, too," replied Marie. "I hope Dad lets us take all this in the car."

They headed back.

When they reached their towel-and-umbrella "beach camp," they found that Mr. and Mrs. Cantu were not alone.

"These are the Murrays," explained Dad.

Mr. Murray reached out his hand. Marie shook it, as did Noelle. Then they shook Mrs. Murray's hand. The sullen boy with them didn't offer his hand.

"Our son left his swim mask and snorkel right here last night," Mr. Murray said. "He just got it for his birthday. We're wondering if you've seen it."

"You're sure it was right here?" Noelle asked.

"We've been coming to this same spot all week," said Mrs. Murray, "so we know it was right here."

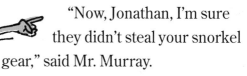

"Did you steal it?" The boy finally spoke.

"Now, Jonathan, I'm sure they didn't steal your snorkel gear," said Mr. Murray.

"Someone did," Jonathan said. "It was probably those boys." He pointed at Marie's brothers, bodysurfing and splashing in the ocean.

"I'm afraid it couldn't have been them," said Mrs. Cantu. "They're our boys, and they came the same time we did. There wasn't any mask or snorkel here when we arrived."

"Maybe someone took it after you left yesterday," suggested Mr. Cantu.

"Or maybe someone took it to the lost and found," said Mrs. Cantu. "Is there a lost and found here?"

"No one picked it up after we left," said Jonathan. "We were here really late. We were the last ones on the beach. And we came here early to get it, before anyone else could." He glared. "But somebody beat us to it."

"Jonathan, that's enough," said Mr. Murray.

"I don't know where the gear is now," Marie said to her parents, "but I think I can identify the thief."

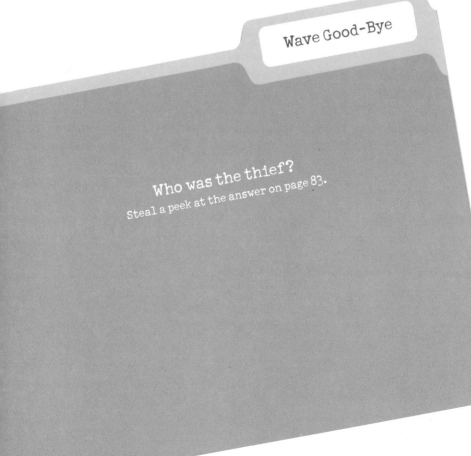

Wave Good-Bye

Who was the thief?
Steal a peek at the answer on page 83.

Garden Party Pooper

A group of girls set out to garden, and now, someone is secretly being a stick-in-the-mud—but who?

"Time for lunch," shouted Mrs. Ferris.

Seven hot, dirty girls laid down their gardening tools and raced for the house.

"But wash up first!"

The girls took turns washing their hands and faces in the Ferrises' bathrooms, and then they gathered around the kitchen table for lunch.

Hard work makes you hungry, and the turkey and cheese sandwiches and fruit salad began to disappear rapidly.

The Ferrises had a huge vegetable garden. And all of those vegetables needed weeding, thinning, and watering. Most of the time Mrs. Ferris and her four daughters—Hailey, Caitlin, Nicole, and Emma—handled the work. Mr. Ferris helped when he was around, which wasn't often. As an international importer, he was usually off traveling to exotic places buying things to bring home and sell.

Sometimes, Mrs. Ferris hired some of the neighbor girls to help out in the garden. That's why, in addition to the Ferris girls, Marie, Noelle, and Brooke were working so hard on this summer Saturday.

"I wish we had a garden," said Marie.

"I'm glad we don't," added Brooke. "I don't mind working once in a while in other people's gardens, but if we had our own, my grandparents would have me in it every day."

"I wish we didn't have a garden," said Caitlin Ferris. "The only thing I like to do is water it."

"That's all you've been doing all morning," said Hailey. "No one's been able to get that hose away from you."

"I like weeding," said Emma, the youngest Ferris.

"You like getting dirty," corrected Hailey.

Marie carried her dishes to the sink. "That was yummy, and now I'm ready to get back to work."

"I'll go with you," said Noelle. "I'm finished, too."

The rest of the girls were still eating and enjoying their break.

"Let's start hoeing the corn," said Marie as they walked out to the garden. "With both of us working, it shouldn't take long."

"Sounds great," Noelle said, "except . . . where are the hoes?"

The girls had left the hoes propped up against the wheelbarrow. But they were no longer there.

Marie and Noelle looked all over the garden, under the tomato plants, behind the beans, everywhere. Then they spread out and searched through the yard. Not one hoe could be found.

Marie and Noelle headed back to the kitchen. Maybe one of the other girls knew what had happened.

"Has anyone seen the hoes?" asked Marie when she reached the kitchen.

"It's missing?" asked Hailey. "Looks like you're out of luck, Caitlin."

"Why am I out of luck?" asked Caitlin. "I hate to hoe."

"Someone must have just put the hoes away somewhere," said Noelle. "Ideas, anyone?"

"My mom might have," said Nicole. "She's always putting things away. Ask her. I think she's in her bedroom."

"I don't think Mom would do that," Hailey replied. "She wants us to finish the work in the garden. How would hiding the hoes help?"

"It was a thief!" shouted Brooke. "Check for prints in the dirt, girls."

"Very funny, Brooke," said Marie, laughing. "But one of you did hide the hoes. Would you please tell us where they are, Caitlin, so that Noelle and I can get back to work?"

Garden Party Pooper

How did Marie know it was Caitlin?
Get all the dirt on page 83.

Sticks and Stones

What will the girls of Acorn Cabin do now?
One of their trail clues doesn't make sense!

"We know it's hot," said Erica, "so we have a little surprise for you." Marie and Noelle listened to the head camp counselor with anticipation. They had been at Camp Veronica Lake for three sweltering days.

Erica nodded to four other counselors, who were standing behind coolers on the far side of the campfire pit. The four, in unison, opened the cooler lids. "Popsicles!" they shouted.

Everyone cheered.

"Have all you want," Erica said. "But wrappers go in the trash, sticks in this bucket. We're going to use them later for a project." She pointed at a bucket near her feet. "And don't feed the squirrels," she added. The camp was full of the cute creatures, all begging for food. They were hard to resist.

At two o'clock, after a break, the girls gathered again at the campfire pit.

"We have something fun for you," said Erica. "A challenge. Each cabin has been assigned a different path through the woods."

As she spoke, she handed a folded piece of paper to one girl from each of the six cabins. "All paths lead to a secret location, where we'll have our next activity. Your cabin counselors have gone ahead and marked your trail. Last cabin group to the end gets dinner cleanup. The paper I gave you tells where your trail begins. Now, go!"

Marie and Noelle were in Acorn Cabin along with Christina, Sarah, and Annika. Christina unfolded the paper. "Behind the latrines." Eww!

The girls headed for the latrines. Behind them they found a trail. At the head of the trail was a star made out of purple-stained Popsicle sticks. "Someone loved grape," said Marie.

Noelle bent down closer to the star. "So that's why they saved the sticks."

The five girls headed down the trail. At the first fork in the path, a Popsicle-stick arrow pointed them to the right.

At the second fork, Popsicle sticks on the right trail spelled "NO." Sticks on the left trail spelled "YES." The girls headed left.

At the third fork, there was a large flat stone. On the stone, Popsicle sticks spelled out "L I F T."

"Lift?" asked Noelle. "We're supposed to lift the rock? It's huge! We can't lift it."

"Let's try," said Sarah. "There must be something under it that tells us where to go next. If all five of us lift, maybe we can move it."

They tried. They failed. The rock wouldn't budge.

"A lever," said Annika, the tallest of the girls. "We're supposed to figure out how to lift the rock. We need to find a lever." The girls looked until they found a long, dead branch. Annika shoved an end under the rock, and the girls all pushed down on the branch.

Snap! The branch broke. The girls tumbled to the ground.

"Maybe we're supposed to lift just the sticks," said Sarah.

"And when we lift the sticks, what?" asked Annika. "The earth will open up, revealing a secret tunnel?"

"No," said Sarah. "But maybe there's something written under them." She lifted the sticks, one by one. Nothing.

"Let's pick a trail and take it," said Annika. "If we just stand here, we're guaranteed to get dinner cleanup. If we pick a trail, we have a fifty-fifty chance of choosing the right one."

"And a fifty-fifty chance of getting lost," said Noelle.

"Look!" said Christina. "I've found it!" She pointed to three sticks that were just lying on the trail to the right. "We're supposed to take the right branch. Let's go."

Marie grabbed her. "Wait." She looked at the sticks on the trail. She looked at the sticks on the stone. "I know what the clue is. I know which way to go."

Sticks and Stones

What is the clue? Which way are the girls to go?

My Summer Vacation

Vacation memories turn into a mystery when the teacher decides to tell her tale.

There are several important things that you're required to do the first day back at school after summer vacation.

You have to find out if you're lucky enough to have some of your friends in your classes (and if you get to sit by them). You have to see if your homeroom teacher is going to be mean or nice. And you have to hear about what everyone did over the summer.

Marie and Noelle met the first requirements. They were in many of the same classes, and their homeroom teacher said they could sit together as long as they didn't disrupt class. They'd convinced her that they should sit together because

they were the new student body president and vice president, and they had to plan.

Brooke and Hailey were also in their class.

Their homeroom teacher, Ms. Toone, seemed very nice (though the girls had learned from past years that a class that goofed off too much could turn a nice teacher mean).

That left summer vacation.

All the kids had had a chance to say what they'd done during the summer. Marie and Noelle told about their beach vacation, about summer camp, and about their first balloon rides.

Hailey told about the trip she'd taken with her father to Brazil.

Brooke described her travels to Boston with her grandfather, who was honored for having played the organ for so many years. The Red Sox team all signed a ball for Brooke's grandfather, who then gave the ball to Brooke.

After everyone described their adventures in detail, Ms. Toone spoke up.

"I did something very exciting this summer, too," said the teacher. "But I'm going to give you some clues and you're going to have to figure out what it was."

Marie and Noelle leaned forward. They loved a challenge.

Ms. Toone continued. "I saw four states in a couple of seconds."

"What did she say?" Marie asked.

"I'm not sure," replied Noelle.

Ms. Toone went on. "I didn't drive through or fly to all four states, though."

"No one can walk that fast!" said Matt. "And time machines haven't been built, yet."

"But the most fun I had," she continued, "is when I pulled out the game Twister and played in all four states at the same time.

Anyone want to guess where I went?"

Marie reached into her desk and pulled out a pocket atlas. She pointed at something on the page for Noelle. Then, Marie's and Noelle's hands shot up.

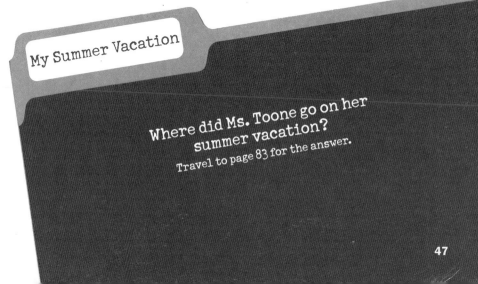

My Summer Vacation

Where did Ms. Toone go on her summer vacation?

Travel to page 83 for the answer.

Chalk One Up

An accident leaves two girls covered in chalk dust.
So why are the girls' friends angry at them?

"Did I wear a jacket this morning?" Noelle asked Marie on their way home from school.

"Yeah," said Marie. "So did I."

"Well, how many of us are wearing jackets right now?"

Marie counted. "One, two . . . zero."

Together Marie and Noelle said, "We left them at school!"

The girls turned and headed back to their homeroom.

As they walked in, two ghosts suddenly appeared in front of them.

"What in the . . ." muttered Marie.

"Faith, Sage, what's going on?" Noelle asked.

Faith and Sage dropped the chalk erasers they were pounding each other with and turned toward the girls. They had guilty looks on their faces. Sage's normally red hair was pink, and Faith's brown hair was gray.

"That's what I want to know," said a voice behind Marie and Noelle. It was Ms. Toone. She didn't wear her usually happy expression.

Ms. Toone walked to the front of the room, followed by Marie and Noelle. Every inch of Ms. Toone's desk, her chair, the map of the United States—and everything else within a four-foot radius—was covered in chalk dust. Even the phone had a smooth, thick layer of chalk dust on it.

"Before two girls get into very serious trouble, they'd better explain what happened," said Ms. Toone.

"It was the chalk vac," said Sage. The "chalk vac" is what Ms. Toone called the mini vacuum cleaner that she let the kids on chalkboard duty use to clean the dust from the chalk tray. "It fell apart and the dust blew all over the place."

"Where is it?" asked Ms. Toone.

Faith reached under Ms. Toone's desk and pulled out the little vacuum. "We put it back together."

Marie and Noelle had been on chalk duty two days ago, and they'd noticed then that the chalk vac would need emptying soon. They could see through the clear plastic of the vacuum that, indeed, it had been emptied—but not into the trash.

"How long ago did this happen?" asked Ms. Toone.

"About ten minutes ago," answered Sage.

"Why didn't you call the office and report it?"

"We did!" said Sage. "But, uh, there wasn't an answer. Then we called again, but it was busy."

"I think if you call now," said Marie to Ms. Toone, "they might answer."

While Ms. Toone made the call, Noelle turned to Sage.

"If you two were so concerned about this mess, why were you having an eraser fight?"

"Hey," said Faith, "once the mess was made, we couldn't resist." Faith shook her hair and a faint wisp of chalk dust floated over to Marie and Noelle.

Noelle sneezed. "Stop that," she said.

"The custodian will be right here," Ms. Toone told the girls. "While we're waiting, let's start cleaning."

Ms. Toone pulled a broom from the closet. Sage checked the chalk vac to make sure it wouldn't fall apart, then started vacuuming.

When the custodian came into the room, he stopped dead in his tracks. He wasn't happy. "What happened here?" he asked.

Sage quickly explained. "We're sorry," said Sage. "It was an accident. And after it happened, we tried right away to get it taken care of. We called the office but couldn't get an answer."

"Well, I don't have time right now to clean it up. I'm in the middle of a couple of other urgent jobs. But you two girls," he pointed to dust-covered Sage and Faith, "can just stay here and clean until I get back. If I think you've done enough, I'll finish up. If not, we'll call your parents and explain to them why you'll be home late."

After the custodian left, Ms. Toone said, "I'm going to the office for some rags. We're going to need them."

Right after Ms. Toone left, Marie looked at the two ghosts. "Sage, this might have started as an accident, but you did not try to take care of it right away. Noelle and I will help you clean up. But Ms. Toone's a really nice teacher, and you shouldn't lie to her."

Chalk One Up

How did Marie know that Sage had been lying?
The truth is on page 83.

Cream Puff Day

Brooke plans to double her desserts but ends up with an empty plate. Where did things go wrong?

"Trade you . . . my peas for your dessert," Marie said to Noelle.

"I'll trade you . . . my peas and my milk for your dessert," Noelle responded.

"I'll trade you . . . our house, our car, and the six million dollars I'm going to make when I'm rich and famous for your dessert," Marie said.

"I'll trade you all that and an old shoe for your dessert," said Noelle.

It was a game they played on Cream Puff Day. Marie and Noelle didn't know how the lunch ladies, whose food was usually O.K. but not special, made their cream puffs so incredible. The girls figured it must just be magic.

And they knew that there was no way that either one of them would trade anything for her cream puff. But the chance to get two cream puffs? Tempting.

Brooke sat down across from them. "Trade you my peas for your cream puffs," she said.

Marie and Noelle laughed.

"You are getting sleepy," said Marie. "You don't want our cream puffs. In fact, you don't even want yours, do you? You are in my power. Now you will hand your cream puff over to me."

Brooke laughed, encircling her cream puff with her arms. She stopped and then smiled. "I'll make you a deal, though." She pulled a pencil from her pocket and tore her napkin in half. "I'm going to mark these two napkin pieces." As she talked, she held each napkin piece under the table where no one could see it, made a quick mark on it, and folded it. "Then I'll give one of you lucky girls the chance to pick one of the pieces. If you pick the piece with the X, you get my cream puff. If you pick the piece with the O, I get your cream puff. Anyone game? Anyone want the chance to have two whole delicious cream puffs at the very same time? You have a fifty-fifty chance!"

Marie looked at Noelle. Noelle looked at Marie. "I'll do it," said Marie before Noelle could say anything.

Brooke held out one napkin piece in each hand. "Pick one."

Marie thought carefully.

"I think it's a trick," Noelle whispered to Marie.

Marie chose the napkin in Brooke's right hand.

She slowly opened it up, holding it so no one could see, and said, "It's an X. You owe me your cream puff." Then she tore the napkin into little pieces and shoved it into her pocket.

"Wait!" said Brooke. "I don't believe you. You didn't show any of us your napkin."

"Oh, sorry," said Marie, and she smiled at Brooke. "But I'll tell you what we can do. You show me your napkin piece, and if it has an O on it, it'll prove mine had an X."

Brooke sighed as she opened up her napkin. On it was an O.

Then Brooke laughed. "That was clever, Marie. Here's your cream puff."

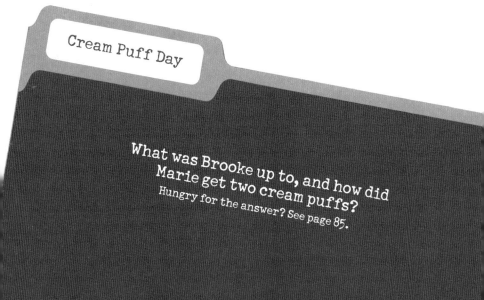

Cream Puff Day

What was Brooke up to, and how did Marie get two cream puffs?
Hungry for the answer? See page 85.

Love Letters

Did the shyest girl in class write a love letter
to one of her classmates?

Rebecca Sorensen was smart. She could name all fifty states
in twenty seconds—thirty seconds if she added the capitals.
She'd been district spelling bee champion two years in a row.
And it wasn't uncommon for Rebecca to correct Ms. Toone
when she made a mistake during math.

But when Rebecca wasn't answering questions, she was
quiet. Rebecca was the shyest kid in class.

So when Brooke found, blown against a bush on the playground, the love letter from Rebecca to Matt, everyone was
surprised.

"Well, I'd never believe it if I didn't see it myself," said Hope.
"Shy Rebecca has a boyfriend!"

"At least she has good taste," said Sage.

"Speak for yourself," Faith said. "Matt burps louder than anyone I've ever heard. It's disgusting."

Hailey grabbed the note and read it out loud:

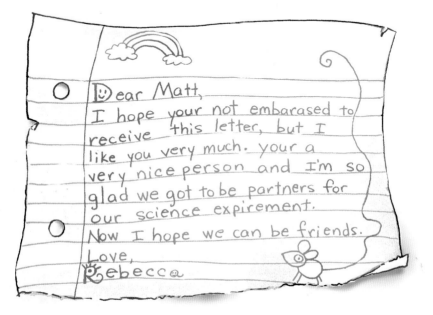

Dear Matt,
I hope your not embarased to receive this letter, but I like you very much. your a very nice person and I'm so glad we got to be partners for our science expirement. Now I hope we can be friends.
Love,
Rebecca

"How sweet!" She held the note to her chest and fluttered her eyelashes.

"Do you think Matt likes her back?" Hope asked.

"Don't see why he wouldn't." It was Noelle's turn to get her two cents in. "She's smart, and she has a nice smile when she's not hiding it."

"Can I see that note?" Marie asked, and she took it from Hailey.

"I can't wait to tell everyone in class. Rebecca likes Matt," Brooke began to sing.

"I don't know if we should be spreading this all over," said Noelle. "I don't think Rebecca wanted anyone to read this note."

"There's an even better reason we shouldn't be spreading this around class," said Marie. "This might be a real note from Rebecca to Matt, but it's not from *our* Rebecca."

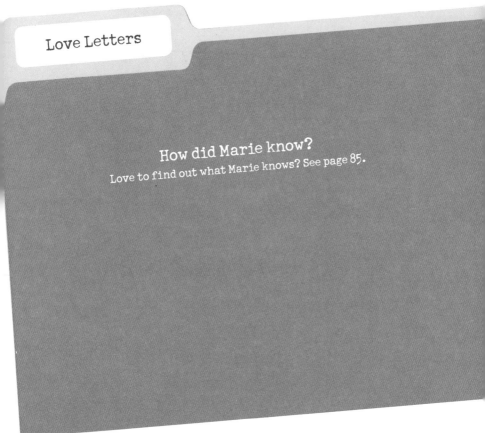

Love Letters

How did Marie know?
Love to find out what Marie knows? See page 85.

Easy as Pie

Someone secretly ate a pumpkin pie. But in a house
filled with people, how will anyone figure out who?

"Junior, get out of the kitchen," Marie said as she shooed out
the family's Scotty dog, then returned to help her mom with
Thanksgiving dinner.

Mom and Marie had made the pies—one pumpkin, two
apple, and one pecan—yesterday. The pies were in the pantry,
where they'd stay until dessert time.

The turkey in the oven was almost ready. The rolls and yams
were done, the table was set, and Marie was finishing up the
mashed potatoes. Dinner would be ready soon.

There would be plenty of it. And there would need to be. Marie's brothers alone could eat most of it. They always seemed to be hungry, especially Chris, who was bigger than Zachary, even though he was two years younger.

And then there was everyone else around the table—Marie's parents, her grandparents, her aunt and uncle and their five kids, and Marie herself. Fifteen people could put away a lot of food. And that wasn't counting Junior, who would get his fill of Thanksgiving leftovers.

Mom pulled the turkey from the oven. It smelled soooo good. "Call everyone in to the dining room, would you, Marie?" she asked.

Marie was happy to oblige. She shouted upstairs to her brothers. "Tyler, Zachary, Chris, time for dinner!" Immediately Tyler and Zachary emerged from Tyler's room and leaped down the stairs, followed by their five cousins. Marie didn't even want to know what kinds of mischief they had been creating.

Marie's father and uncle poked their heads in from the living room. "Did we hear right? Do we finally get to eat?" Dad asked. "Mmmm, that turkey smells good."

The kids and Marie's grandparents found their seats. Marie's dad, mom, uncle, and aunt were soon seated, and finally her brother Chris pulled up his chair and sat down.

Each person said what he or she was thankful for, and then the feast began.

Dad carved the turkey.

Tyler and Zachary scooped huge piles of mashed potatoes onto their plates.

The cousins soon had their plates filled, too.

Chris took a piece of turkey and some cranberry sauce.

Grandma and Grandpa waited patiently to serve themselves until their grandchildren had begun to eat.

Marie picked a piece of turkey off her plate and reached it down to Junior under the table. "There's more where that came from," she told the excited dog. "And leave room for pie." Junior loved pumpkin pie.

As soon as the moans and groans about full stomachs had begun, Mom announced, "I'm ready for dessert. Who wants pie?"

A chorus of cheers erupted.

"Marie, would you help me?"

When Marie and her mother reached the pantry, Mom looked at the pies, frowned, and asked, "Didn't we make four pies?"

"Two apple, a pumpkin, and a pecan," Marie said.

"Well now, it looks as if the pie bandits have been here. We're missing a pumpkin pie."

Mom left the pies in the pantry, and she and Marie returned to the dining room.

"We have a mystery," Mom said. "Marie and I made four pies. Now there are only three. One pie is missing. Any idea where it went?"

"I'll bet Marie ate it," said her brother Zachary. "She couldn't resist."

"Have you checked Junior's hiding spots?" Marie's brother Chris asked. "He's been in the kitchen, hasn't he? And we know how much he loves pumpkin pie."

Everyone looked down at Junior, who was so sure he had done something wrong again that he slunk under the table.

Marie's uncle looked at his kids. "What were you kids all doing up in Tyler's room? I predict that a careful inspection will reveal an empty pie plate hidden under the bed."

One of the cousins spoke up. "I predict that careful inspection will reveal an empty pie plate hidden under the sofa in the living room where the grown-ups were watching football."

"I think it's pretty clear who ate the pie," Marie said.

"Clear to me, too," Mom said. She smiled. "On the count of three, if you know who ate the pie, point to the culprit. One . . . two . . . three!"

Marie and Mom both pointed to the same person.

Easy as Pie

Who took the pie,
and how did Marie and her mom know?
Don't let it eat at you. See page 85.

Lost in the Library

Why would someone hide Lincoln Middle School's most popular book—in the library?

"*Harriet Putter!* It's in! Oh, I want it next!" Marie clutched the book and looked at Mrs. Morris, the school librarian. *Harriet Putter,* the story of a girl with magical powers, was the hottest thing at Lincoln Middle School.

Brooke grabbed for it. "No, Marie, that book has my name written all over it. I get it next."

"Your name? It has my name and I get it."

"We'll see who gets it," said Brooke. "Mrs. Morris, since I'm your favorite library aide and since I'm working in the library now and Marie's just hanging out, I get *Harriet Putter,* don't I?"

"I'd love to let both of you have it, but you know the rules," sighed Mrs. Morris. "It goes to the next person on the waiting list. Have you two signed up?"

"Days ago," Marie said. "And I'm still twelfth on the list."

"I'm eleventh on the list," Brooke said. "Ha! I get it first."

"After ten other people," Marie said.

"Maybe, maybe not."

"I've ordered more copies, girls," Mrs. Morris said. "When they come in, you'll move up the list more quickly. In the meantime, leave the book with me and get to class. The bell's about to ring. Brooke, back to work. Marie, I'll see you at two."

Marie was scheduled to work that afternoon as a library aide.

At two o'clock sharp Marie was back in the library for her class hour as an aide. "Shelve these books for me, would you?" asked Mrs. Morris. "They all go in the science section."

Marie pushed the book cart over to the corner where the science books were located and began to put books on the shelves where they belonged: a book about space, one about nuclear energy, one about lizards ... what was this? *Harriet Putter?* In the science section? She pulled it off the shelf and took it up to Mrs. Morris.

"It was between *Lizards of Albania* and *Lizards of the Arctic*," said Marie. "How do you think it got there?"

"It didn't get there by magic," said Mrs. Morris. "I'll ask at our library aides meeting tomorrow."

"I thought you had a conference and were going to have a substitute."

"That was the plan, but they cancelled the conference, so here I'll be. See you tomorrow morning."

In the morning Mrs. Morris told the aides to have a seat. There were seven aides: three boys—Matt, Nate, and Russell—and four girls—Marie, Faith, Brooke, and Hope.

"Yesterday, somehow, *Harriet Putter* was moved from my desk, where I had it saved for Allie Bentley, who was next on the list to check it out," said Mrs. Morris. "It ended up on the shelves. Does anyone have any idea how it got there?"

"I wasn't at school yesterday," explained Russell.

"It wasn't my day to help," said Hope.

"I was here yesterday," said Brooke. "I shelved the whole time in the fiction section, but I left the book on your desk. Didn't touch it. Promise."

"I was here, too," said Matt. "But I was shelving in the history section, not the science section. I couldn't have put it there."

"I came in yesterday to check out a book," said Nate, "but my day to shelve is tomorrow."

"And today's my day," said Faith.

"Well, keep an eye out, and be careful when you're shelving," said Mrs. Morris. "We don't want this accident repeated, however it happened. And we don't want to lose a book as popular as *Harriet Putter.*"

It wasn't an accident, Marie thought to herself. She didn't tell this to Mrs. Morris, though. She just glanced over at the person in the group she knew had put the book on the shelf and smiled.

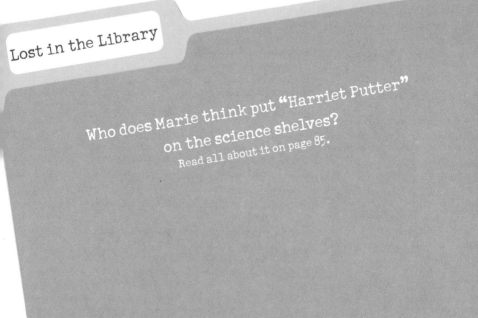

Lost in the Library

Who does Marie think put "Harriet Putter" on the science shelves?

Read all about it on page 85.

Win, Lose, or Draw

A silly drawing is discovered by the teacher,
and she knows who did it. Or does she?

"Step up, one and all, and sign Ms. Toone's birthday card,"
Marie shouted to the class. Ms. Toone had left the room for a
few minutes to run errands. She'd instructed the class to work
quietly on math until lunch, but Marie thought that a birthday
was a good reason for a little commotion.

All the students in the class came over and signed the card.

"What happened to your arm, Russell?" Marie asked.
Russell's right arm, elbow to fingertips, was in a cast, cradled
in a sling.

"An elephant fell on it," said Russell.

"Knowing you," added Noelle, "you probably tripped the
elephant."

The students worked on their assignments until the lunch
bell rang. While kids rushed out of the classroom, Marie set
the birthday card on Ms. Toone's desk and headed off to the
lunchroom.

The next day, the students returned to Ms. Toone's class.
Once they were at their desks and had quieted down, class
began.

"I would like to thank you all for your kind birthday card," said Ms. Toone. Marie and Noelle smiled.

"And I would also like to thank a very fine artist who is hiding in our class. When I came in yesterday after this class, I found on the floor a beautiful, anonymous portrait of myself." She held up a drawing of a fish writing on a chalkboard. "Let me read the caption for those of you who can't see it. It says, 'Ms. Tuna in her fish school'."

The kids laughed.

Ms. Toone looked around the room. "I want to know who drew this picture."

The laughter quieted. Was Ms. Toone angry? She wasn't smiling as much as usual.

"I did find it under one of your desks," she said. "One of the boys' desks." She walked around the room, peering at each of the students as though she were a lawyer in a murder trial. "And the desk I found it under was . . . yours!" She turned quickly and pointed at Russell.

Russell jumped, and everyone laughed. "I didn't do it!" said Russell. "I couldn't have. Look." He held up his broken arm.

"Oh, Russell, Russell, Russell," said Ms. Toone. "How vehemently the guilty do protest."

Marie smiled. She now realized that Ms. Toone was playing with Russell. She whispered something quickly to Noelle.

Noelle stood up. "Madam teacher," she said. "I confess."

The class turned to Noelle expectantly.

Noelle continued. "I confess that Russell did it."

"Well, well, well," said Ms. Toone. "Seems we have a witness. Tell us exactly what you saw, Miss Dee."

Marie stood. "Noelle and I are both witnesses to evidence that Russell could easily have committed this horrible crime."

Some of the kids figured out that a game was in progress. The rest of the class seemed confused, waiting to see Ms. Toone lecture Russell about respect.

"And would you, Miss Cantu, please explain to us just what your evidence is?"

"As the court orders, Ms. Toone. Ladies and gentlemen, our evidence is this . . ."

Win, Lose, or Draw

What was Marie's evidence?
The verdict is in! See page 85.

Sweet Rose

Why would Rose leave a private photo in a library book for all to see? That's what she wants to know!

"Look what I found!" Brooke marched into the classroom holding a photograph above her head.

It was lunchtime. Normally the girls would have been outside after lunch, but because there was a blizzard blowing, the principal had given the students three choices: play in the gym, read in the library, or stay quietly in their homerooms. Marie, Noelle, and Rose had decided to stay in their homeroom and help decorate a bulletin board for Ms. Toone.

"Let me guess," said Rose. "It's a picture of your lovey-dovey boyfriend."

"Oh, so close," said Brooke. "It's a picture of *your* lovey-dovey boyfriend. And I quote from the back of the photo: 'Roses are red, violets are blue, You are sweet and kind, too. Love, Samuel'."

Rose screamed, dove over a desk, leaped at Brooke, and grabbed the photo from her hand. "Where did you get this?"

"I found it," said Brooke.

"Yeah, you found it," said Rose, her face flushed. "You found it in my desk."

"Did not," said Brooke, smiling. "I found it in the library, in a book."

"It was in my desk!"

"No, really, I found it in a library book. It was in a copy of *Harriet Putter* that had just come in. It was between pages 99 and 100."

"Between 99 and 100?" asked Noelle. "You remember the exact page numbers?"

"Yeah," said Brooke. "Funny, huh. I thought it was interesting that the picture was between pages 99 and 100. That's why I remembered them."

"What would my picture be doing in a library book?" asked Rose.

"I don't know," replied Brooke. "Maybe somebody else took it and hid it there. Maybe she left it there as a bookmark. Or, since you just finished reading *Harriet Putter,* maybe you left the picture there. I can see it now—you read a page, you look at Samuel, you read a page, you look at Samuel—ah, romance. Rose has one true love."

"He's not my *one* true love."

"Oh, you have more than one true love?" teased Brooke.

"I don't have *any* true loves," said Rose. "He's just a friend."

"A friend who signs with 'love'?" asked Brooke. "It's O.K., Rose. You can have a true love. We understand. You were reading with the photo, you forgot to take it out, and you returned the book. Simple. Case closed."

"Case closed, all right," said Marie. "Stop teasing Rose and come clean. You took the picture, and that's why you're lying to Rose about where you got it."

Sweet Rose

How did Marie know that Brooke was lying?

Picture the answer, then check page 85.

The Governor Is Calling

Someone's making prank calls—and Marie knows who!
What should she do now?

"May I speak with Marie Cantu?" the voice on the phone asked.

"This is Marie," answered Marie.

"Please hold for the governor."

Marie looked at the phone. Why would the governor be calling her? She waited for the governor to speak. She did help out at the animal shelter every weekend. And then there were her honors in English. Had she saved anyone's life lately?

She thought about these things as she waited . . . and waited . . . and waited. Finally, she realized the truth. Someone had played a trick on her!

She hung up the phone.

It rang again. Marie answered it. "Ha ha ha! Very funny," she said into the phone.

"Marie?" It was Noelle. "I've been trying to call you for fifteen minutes, but your line was busy."

"Oh hi, Noelle. I just got a prank call. I thought it was the same person trying to call me again."

"The governor?"

"The governor," said Marie. "She called you, too? I waited for fifteen minutes before hanging up."

"I waited twenty minutes. Beat you," said Noelle. "Who do you think it was?"

"She disguised her voice, but now that I think about it, it sounded like Megan."

"I think we need to plan a little revenge. I'll be right over."

The girls discussed options, then headed over to Megan's house.

It had been snowing all morning, and when Marie and Noelle reached Megan's, a blanket of snow covered the lawn, the sidewalk, everything. The girls walked up the sidewalk,

making footprints in the spotless snow.

Marie whispered to Noelle. Noelle nodded. Then they went to work. Quietly they rolled snow into large balls. Together they pushed and heaved the balls up onto Megan's porch and built a large snowman, right in front of the door.

Then they rang the doorbell and ran to hide behind the next-door neighbor's bushes.

Megan opened the door. "What's this?" she asked. She tried to push the screen door open. It moved just a few inches, then hit the snowman and would go no farther.

A few minutes later Megan emerged from behind the house. She stomped onto the porch and began to dismantle the snowman.

"Hi, Megan!" said Noelle. She and Marie walked up Megan's sidewalk as though they had just arrived. "Why are you building a snowman on your porch? Aren't you afraid it will block your door?"

"Very funny," said Megan. "I owe you one."

"No, we're even," said Marie. "So, how's the governor?"

"The governor? I don't know what you're talking about."

Marie told her about the prank calls.

"You think I made them?" asked Megan. "I wish. But I didn't. I walked over to the library this morning to work on my research report on Peru. I just got back ten minutes ago. Help me get this snowman off the porch, and we can go inside and get some hot cocoa."

Marie and Noelle helped Megan roll the rest of the snowman away from the door. Then the girls went in, sipped hot cocoa, and talked.

After awhile, Marie stood up. "I'd better get going." Noelle stood, too.

The girls started to leave. Then Marie turned back and said, "So tell me, Megan, who else did you call? Just us?"

"I told you, I didn't call you," said Megan.

"Oh, I think you did," said Marie. "You didn't go to the library today. I think you were here all morning being the governor's secretary."

The Governor Is Calling

How did Marie know that Megan hadn't gone to the library?

The answer is calling you on page 87.

Who Hearts Who

What happens when a box of chocolates
turns into a logic problem of love?

Marie scanned the classroom, looking for chocolate
hearts—not just any chocolate hearts, but special, expensive
chocolate hearts from Switzerland.

Hailey's dad had brought a big box of them back from his last trip and had given several to each of his daughters. Hailey had decided to share.

On one condition.

Marie, Noelle, and Brooke could each have a chocolate if they promised to also give one in their valentine to a boy in class they liked. "I'll give one, too," said Hailey.

The chocolate looked so good. The plan was tempting.

"But I don't love any of the boys in our class!" Brooke said. "Matt's not bad, and neither is Russell. I wouldn't mind giving a chocolate heart to one of them. But I don't love them."

"I didn't say you have to love them," Hailey said. "This isn't saying you want them to be your boyfriend. Just give the heart to the boy you like the most."

"But then he'll think I want to be his girlfriend," said Noelle.

"Send it anonymously," said Hailey. "No one will ever know who you sent your heart to."

"But he'll figure out who it is," said Brooke. "We have to give valentines to everyone in class, and if some boy gets one unsigned valentine, and he figures out that I'm the only one who didn't send a signed valentine, he'll know it's from me."

"Hey," said Marie. "First, I don't think he's going to think that a chocolate heart means someone loves him. He's just going to think it's cool, and then he'll eat it. Second, even if he thinks it's a love message, I doubt he'll make the effort to figure out who didn't send a valentine. And third, even if he does, just give him two different valentines—one signed without chocolate, one unsigned with chocolate."

It was a plan.

The girls had kept secret—even among themselves—who they were giving their chocolates to.

This made Marie curious.

She looked around the classroom. There was Matt with a chocolate, and Russell had one. Who else——yes, Ben was pulling one of the chocolates out of an envelope. That left one more. Or did one of the boys get two chocolates? No, Nate was holding one up and looking at it hungrily.

Now, who gave chocolate to whom?

She knew one for sure. She'd given hers to Matt.

And she knew who Brooke liked.

She also knew Noelle wouldn't have given hers to Nate. Noelle didn't like Nate.

She drew a grid on a piece of paper.

💙	Brooke	Noelle	Hailey	Marie
Matt				
Nate				
Russell				
Ben				

And soon she knew which girl had given a chocolate to which boy.

Then she began opening her valentines. Maybe someone had given chocolate to her.

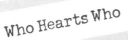
Who Hearts Who

Which boy had each girl given to?
Wouldn't it be sweet to know? See page 87.

Wishing for Change

Behind the Door

Play with Your Feud

An Elephant for President?

Rock and Rumors

Up, Up, and A-What?

The Original
Boston Brooke

Wave Good-Bye

Garden Party
Pooper

Sticks and Stones

My Summer
Vacation

Chalk One Up

Cream Puff Day

Love Letters

Easy as Pie

Lost in the Library

Win, Lose, or Draw

Sweet Rose

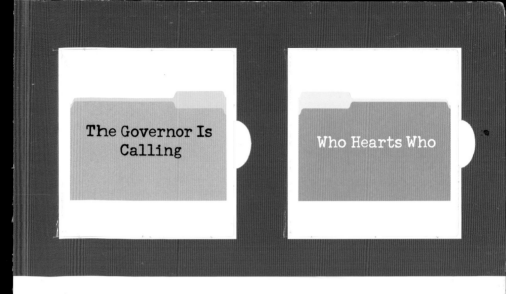

The Governor Is Calling

Who Hearts Who

Did you like these mysteries?
Would you like some more?
Let us know!

Send your comments to:

Mini Mysteries Editor
American Girl
8400 Fairway Place
Middleton, WI 53562